Peter Cron who chatters about ZVI.

Hélène Binet

בכא

חלבבית

1.2.99

London

HOU

JSE OF

BUILDING
ZVI HECKER
PHOTOGRAPHS
HELENE BINET
TEXT
PETER COOK
JOHN HEJDUK
ZVI HECKER

THE BO

PUBLISHED BY
BLACK DOG
PUBLISHING
LIMITED

ISBN
1 901033 15 5

OK

ZVI HECKER'S JEWISH SCHOOL IN BERLIN

PETER COOK

We are in the presence of a simultaneously overt and covert object. The school appears to declare its preoccupations immediately, the plan being perceptible as a whirling flower. Yet it demands an analysis that bypasses both the traps of preoccupation with the historical and the moral; the significance of reinvesting a Jewish presence in Berlin and the quite different trap of quizzing Hecker's formal and generic mannerisms. It is a tantalisingly difficult building for the late 20th-century eye: for we have become conditioned (unwittingly?) by the televisual image that carries with it any number of homogenisations and distillations so that the visual language of architecture is often found wanting. No wonder that architect-intellectuals attempt to bypass the issue by selling out the visual tradition as inferior to that of 'content', 'meaning' or non-visual language. Unfortunately for them, Hecker's school is thrusting, accosting even, refusing to let you rest upon some easy explanation of the plan figure: for its obvious richness lies in the moments when this exploding gyratory system allows incursions, flicks-across or shavings-away to happen.

Yet in the televisual post-wall period, Berlin itself is beginning to move in the same direction as Adelaide or Mannheim: the city street taking on the character of middle-income clothing stores where the fashions send out reassuring signals, "I'm a respecter of old values but I'm efficient" … or "I'm friendly but just a little bit trendy too". Meanwhile, its suburbs crave their own place in this 'sitcom' situation. Fun and games you may have within, but respectability at all costs, please, towards the street. In the days of the divided city an embarrassing game of ideologies, cultures and economies was tossed back and forth across the divide. A piece of "look no hands!" roof on one side, and a piece of pious social responsibility on the other, has now been replaced in the newly rebuilt centre by a series of grim, rigid grids and stony nostalgia. Yet there is *still* something of the old, experimental Berlin in the air: occasional wit seen in competition projects; the continual seeming and being of gurus and bright young observers—a factor that has contributed to Hecker's marvellous 'second wind' as a designer. In Tel Aviv, his other city, he was generally treated as an eccentric and an artist, a perfectionist in an architectural culture of the cut creative corner. Added to which, he perhaps instinctively craved the presence of a serious peer group: other architects and talkers-about-architecture with whom he could debate the nuances and implications of a design, rather than just its politics or symbolism.

The attention to detail in the Jewish School is the result of this rediscovered climate: where to discuss the position of the window frame, the degree of 'cut' in a 'cut', the necessity (or otherwise) of an articulated edge. The syncopation of a consistent run of, say, openings. Are these things mannerist issues, or are they the *stuff* of architecture? In comparing the school with the spiral housing in Ramat Gan, Israel, you can of course attribute them both to the same author. In Berlin, the sunflower explodes across the ground, whereas the house has to climb upwards as it explodes. The power of horizontal shards is common to both: equally skilful strokes that many architects would be too afraid to posit. In both cases they act as giant 'clips' or as exploded architraves. Yet in each context, they have a virtuoso ability to both attack and underscore the dynamics of the building. In matters of content and rhetoric the two buildings have some fascinating overtones. The Ramat Gan site is opposite Hecker's own home, which is no mere professional's suburban villa—he lives in the Dubliner apartments that he designed together with Alfred Neumann and Eldar Sharon in 1961, a successful essay in interlock geometry that is able to leap across space and simultaneously hover over its hillside site. The spiral is the unruly child opposite, hairy and jagged, whereas Dubliner is made of more consistent material: concrete, of course. A geometric system initiates them both, but the heroics are quite contrary: for the first building, a demonstration of logic, commodity and evenness; 22 years later the need is for freedom, the chance to delight in the power of architecture to not only capture space, but also leap into it. The chosen surface material is now a 'cheapo' stone appliqué used more often by local Arab builders and having quite kitschy overtones, in itself enough to raise the eyebrows of a bourgeois suburb. The implications are of glass and mosaic, as well as the proliferation of displaced 'frame' conditions, and all this before we come to the power and originality of the plan itself.

What is this man about? How did he simmer away in Tel Aviv, making one building every few years, talking mostly to painters and sculptors, with an enviable library that kept him aware of explosions elsewhere?

The Berlin building owes much to Ramat Gan: those detached frames reappear, but as elegant and finely-tuned markers, without which the flat flanks would remain too diagrammatic. It reminds one of his continual ability to set 'stages', conditions in which the appearance of people—a terrible bore to many abstractionist architects—are positively desirable. There are innumerable crevices, stages 'off', shadow flanks and hidden layers from which kids or visitors can suddenly emerge. His delight in creating the snake-ways that interfere with the central sunflower theme is the delight of a designer who is completely in control of the situation. The snakes have an ironic quality, appearing to be anarchic elements, but quite immaculately placed, having their own system and logic, appearing and disappearing quickly, needing in *this* building to be deft and neat.

It could all be the playing-out of a long cycle of rediscovery. The young Hecker arrived in Israel as a second-year student from Krakow into an energetic Haifa Technion during the period of Alfred Neumann: not only his teacher, but his first partner. A scenery of jagged concrete knives appearing out of the scrub lands of the Eastern Mediterranean: some contrast indeed to the nervous and pared down paranoia of Catholic-Socialist interplay that he had left behind. The fascination with the geometries and the repetition of geometric elements (often precast) is an undeniable inheritance that cannot entirely be explained away by the fascination of Eastern patterning meeting single-edge constructability. Wolfgang Pehnt suggests that Zvi Hecker, Alfred Neumann and their third partner, Elder Sharon "fought geometry, the simple norm with the complicated one". Having watched Hecker scraping away on his plans, I would add that he can now fight geometry with that craft-associated process of 'honing'. The silvers, tweaks and pats that he gives to the stated thrusts lead on to the process of incursion and the deliberate planting of alien elements that in the end serve to strengthen the audacity of the original thrust. Hecker sits on the site, endlessly producing more drawings, wandering round the building cogitating upon possible tweaks that will clarify the communication of the idea. Only Gunther Domenly in his 'B Bank' period has come close to this degree of involvement.

What we see at this site on the edge of Grunewald is therefore a building that can neither play the set game of urban heroics of modern Berlin (although it is a large building) nor play the coy suburban decorum of many school buildings. It suggests that though children are sweet, they are adventurous too, they need a 'place', not just a well-meaning set of boxes. All the classrooms are at least *slightly* different. The stairs are easy to find, but where they lead will always have local idiosyncracies. Certain pieces of wall will be unfinished, certain paths of light will come from unexpected sources, certain window sills will reveal themselves to be secret balconies.

Hecker has moved a long way from his colleagues from the Technion who seem to be content to set up a geometrical gambit and then let it run 'clack, clack, clack, clack' down to the end of the building and then stop, somewhat startled. He has a passionate fascination for the formative act, so he interferes with the generic sunflower motif and produces a building (the Palmach Centre in Tel Aviv) where a climbing rampart system is attached—geometrically—only once and in the new Jewish Cultural Centre at Duisberg the 'frame' members have graduated to the category of primary 'carriers' of the building. It is an architecture in full flight: creating and recreating itself from the confident observation of form, as it both seduces and attends space. Helene Binet's photographs of the school are the first that seem to understand the complex three-dimensionality of the building. It is not dependent on its (fairly obvious) challenging 'shapes'. It is more than a series of 'A-B-A-B' shards and recesses and the naughtinesses have to be seen referentially in scale with the total building.

Coming through is a final piquancy: for the Mediterranean experience is there, too. It is not a European building; even if its manners are. The urbanism—and it is surely a piece of urban design in its complexity, hierarchies and the linguistic range of its spaces—is that of a village or even a small town. The left flank, which abuts a straight edged path, has all the wit of a defended or seaside town peeking out from time to time towards the hostile world and allowing occasional (rather diagonal) incursion. This is my own favourite stretch—but then, I'm English.

Village aspects are declared towards the street and, again, a blue-skied day can give the composition a remarkable transportation to those same scrub lands and hillsides upon which his earlier buildings hovered. But it is just a momentary reminder. Hecker's language and very considerable sophistication reaches the level of the best Japanese contrivers, but with more originality and dare. With this building, he has become an essential part of that coterie of architects who are answering back both the televisual and the abstracted world.

SUNFLOWER: SNAKE: PERSEPHONE: BERLIN

JOHN HEJDUK

I. Zvi Hecker's recently completed Jewish Community school in Berlin
    must be considered one of the major works in our time for its *thought-
    provoking* energy that makes us think deep about many things related
    to life and architecture, not least about the meaning of knowledge,
    expulsion, place and death.

    Hecker's architectural plan of the Jewish School is unique in our time,
    it cuts into the heart of what matters. Surely it is about the renewal of
    hope, as it is surely about the inner anguish that brings us face to face
    with the past and the impact of the enormity of the loss. This work of
    Hecker's has the joy of innocence, at first, yet it is *shedding* architecture.

It sheds its first skin, or is in the process of doing so, *in Berlin*. It is a sister of Zvi's Spiral Apartment House. In Israel where the process is one of peeling, one building relative to the north, one building relative to the south; the south about sunflowers, the north about the presence of the snake. Hecker sees the light of the sunflower and the dark of the snake.

II. The first time my wife and I crossed the Berlin Wall into the then East Germany it was with a fair amount of trepidation. We were certainly disturbed and uneasy as we passed by a prison where the prisoners were shouting at the street's passers-by. It was grey. The buildings, the sky, the people, grey.

When we entered the museum there and were confronted with the Pergamon Hellenistic marble friezes, I was stunned. There were many snakes within the work. Man and snake. Those images have never left me. The writhing of the snakes and men.

We then proceeded to the room where Persephone was. To *see* her, impregnated our souls. The light in the room had a grey mist. You could see the particles of air at times giving off an opaque crystal light. Persephone was in a contained room in Berlin. A year or two later we returned to gaze at her again, but she was no longer in the room, it was empty ... had she returned from the Underworld to her beloved homeland, far to the Southeast? Her departure left a feeling of foreboding.

During the same year we were able to visit the Archaeological Museum in Athens. We arrived almost at closing time and few people were left in that haunting place. We looked at the sarcophagi which were surrounded by sculptures of the dead mother, father, and child, domestic animals and strange winged creatures—man and beast. The conclusion I came to was that these creatures were simply unimaginable. They, too, as the mother, father, child ... *were*.

In Solopaca, Italy, in 1953, I walked up a hill covered in olive trees with my wife's eighty-year-old uncle; we started down the hill on stone stairs. On one side was a high descending stone wall, on the other side, the olive trees. Suddenly in front of our path a large black snake slithered in front of our feet. I was taken aback. I said to Uncle America: "Did you see that snake?" He replied: "What snake?" I answered "The one that just crossed our path." He said "No, I did not." In amazement I said: "How could you possibly not have seen such a large snake?" He calmly replied " I do not believe in snakes."

A friend of mine who is an anthropologist related an ancient phenomenon where one of the gods becomes an immense monumental snake that eventually swallows up everything in the world, even the air. I thought to myself that that god snake had swallowed up everything outside in ... nothing left ... nothing to fear. The exact opposite of living life and of understanding its sacredness.

III.   Some aspects of Zvi Hecker's Jewish School that I wish to touch upon are his initial sketches, black and white and coloured, his technical black and white plans and the axonometric, the built building, and the problems of photographing such a work. As well as the programme and some thoughts on its possible underlying meaning.

Before I go into the above thoughts, let me make a brief observation about Zvi Hecker's spiral apartment building in Ramat Gan, Israel. No doubt about it, I believe this architectural work to be one of the rare buildings of our time. First, it is one of the few Cubist buildings ever to be built. And it is from the Garden of Eden. When asked about its meaning Zvi alludes that it perhaps has something to do with Paradise. I think it has to do with the concept of peeling. It is like taking an apple and in one continuous knife-cut peeling the skin off—for a split second the apple appears white, then quickly begins to fade to another, darker colour. The inner core of the apartment building is like the apple, a hard core of rough stone and inner planar fin-like flying structures with amazing reflective mirror panels (the reflective seeds). The outside wall of the curving spiral is smooth stuccoed, revealing exposed stone frame openings, and stone wall ledges. Yet once the apple is bitten some agony is to be expected, for the building is literally punctured with planes of metal shafts partially serving as external balconies (heads of piercing arrows). The building remains as stoic as paintings of a martyred saint's body filled with arrows. On one of the building's ledges (of rough stone) there appear to be petrified stone snakes taking in the sun. Antoni Gaudi was equally interested in snakes within architecture. While visiting Paestum in 1953 late one afternoon I saw a snake resting on the top of one of the temple's capitals. After all these years it never occurred to me until now how it got there.

IV. Zvi Hecker's arrival in Berlin to construct
the Jewish School was a lifetime's journey
from Poland to Samarkand, to Kracow,
to Israel and then to Germany. Another
journey form Poland to Israel, then to
America, then back to Europe, and on
to Berlin was taken by Daniel Libeskind
who is presently constructing the Jewish
Museum in Berlin. The Jewish Museum
and the Jewish School are the most
significant and creative works built in
Berlin in recent times. They bear witness
to the indomitable spirit of a people.
Daniel Libeskind's Museum is a lightning
bolt signalling through architecture
the sacredness of life and its mystery.
Zvi Hecker's School, at another end of
the city, is the celebration of learning,
education and hopeful hearts. That
these two men came to be in this place at
the same moment is cause for serious
thought about predestination.

V.   Zvi Hecker's Jewish School is an architecture of shedding and more. Zvi insists on the word *precision* regarding the building. And precise it is. Also it has clarity, sharpness along with perfection in detail. The programme is impeccable. These equalities are to be expected from an artist such as Zvi Hecker. I appreciate these qualities, but there is more, *the hidden*. For *the hidden* we must go to the sketches and the extraordinary coloured/pencil drawings. It is in their depth of evolving thought that lies, I think, the deepest of soul-meaning. These drawings present us with the workings of a mind as it creates. They reveal the psyche and the revelations within its struggle to unearth, to search, to discover. Zvi refers to the plan as a sunflower. It can be that, but in Berlin it is more and possibly otherwise. In plan there is the snake moving through the sunflower petals. There, too, is the snake in the garden. The explosive coloured sketches, the line drawings of the overwhelming movement of the snake as it startles. Zvi draws and renders the petals and snake over and over again. He is obsessive and appears to be exorcising something throughout—out of his drawings. He begins to erase parts of the connecting snake with the educational volume. His coloured drawings are filled with fire, blood and darkness. It is his struggle to cleanse. Originally there was no snake in the plans, then its appearance, then its movement through the plans, through the pages of the house of the book. The former sunflower petals become knife blades, the curved triangles places of learning, they *cut and segment* the snake out of the learning space. Architecture and knowledge kill the snake. Its outside remains as a memory of past evil-doings but it remains. It must be remembered, not forgotten. The sun beats down on its metallic empty skin as remains. I have said this building is about shedding but also solidly fixing memory. The expulsion and killing of a people can never be permitted or tolerated. Zvi Hecker's anguished drawings serve as a warning, hidden at first in his internal/eternal book. The blades can metamorphose back into the sunflower petals as expressed in the built work in the enclosed garden in Berlin.

The subtlety of Zvi Hecker's mind and the mastery of his discipline is first expressed in the black ink drawings of his plans and of the axonometric of the building. *There is nothing like these plans of this axonometric.* One of the most radical plans is presented as a gift to the public. It is one of the most dynamic, kinetic, riveting plans in the history of architecture. The organisation of the plan is brilliant, *precise*, and exhilarating. The precision which Zvi speaks of is also in the plan. Every student of architecture should study these black ink drawings and the axonometric, also the coloured sketches. In the built work the five curved wedge volumes moving around a centre are like five land-ships ploughing through a sea of earth to their destination, a centre of learning. There should be a well in the central section of the site where the seeds of thought can be dropped into the water, mixing together for the birth of new thought.

The five curved wedges are themselves shedding. They attempt to shed their skin of the past. They leave shedded metal structures, we can see the metal trusses shedding their encasements. The tall metal columns supporting the horizontal free buttresses exposed to wind, sun, rain, snow, night and day. These floating structures are the first shedding. The wedges close to the land-ships near the ground produce a second peeling, a second shedding takes place, making way for the birth of a pure white prow, for the whiteness is the innocence of children learning ... to be free.

Within the triangular volume there is a classroom where the wedge triangle shape exaggerates the diminishing internal perspective, an inversion takes place. The last school desk in this room is placed in the apex of the triangle. As the triangle widens forward to the end of the triangle (where the teacher must be), the desks increase in number from the distant apex. The faces ... most students facing the teacher are in the front of the class. The teacher overlooks the sea of faces and sees in the distant apex a single child, the last one. Behind the child is the vanishing point.

Zvi Hecker has created a master work, a house of the book. Perhaps sometime in the future the present fence surrounding the school's site might metamorphose into a wall of books, two books thick; one side, the outside public space, for the outer reading; the other side, the inside exterior garden space of the school for inner reading. I have studied and read Zvi Hecker's book and I thank him for his gift to humanity and to the children most of all.

PART II   Through her photography, Helene Binet searches for the soul within architecture. This is a difficult task, one that requires utmost perseverance, precision and concentration. But more is demanded: does the architectural work looked upon have a soul, and how can the photograph reveal its essence? Can the photographer enter into a communion with the synapsis of a fleeting soul-thought and record its existence in the two-dimensional surface of a still photograph which captures the extraordinary moment of a complete silence? A pregnant silence, which announces that one is in the presence of a soul-sound. The great photographers, such as Helene Binet, hear through their eyes and their patience. They wait for the miraculous vibration. They taste the air change. They anticipate the coming. Their eyes become extended, elongated rays probing within the projected waves, touching the essential source, like the two fingers in Michelangelo's *Creation of Adam* where he showed us that the possibility existed of an expanded abundance in concentrated, compacted forms of spirit.

Zvi Hecker's Jewish School in Berlin is abundant in spirit and meaning, and I believe Helene Binet, through her photographs, has made a sounding into its heart of memory regarding life and death. Zvi Hecker's architecture and Helene Binet's photography of the Jewish School in Berlin brought forth certain questions. The first part of this paper explained what the architecture of Zvi Hecker provoked within my thoughts, the second part, the fact of the built architecture and the photography of the built work led me down an unexpected path: the issue of built architecture as fact, programmatic reality, and the thought that past events and horrendous past tragedies are in the built architecture's memory. Also the question as to where does this reveal itself and the possibility that certain Binet photographs of the built work bring forth the memory of the past. The photograph of the architecture recalls the memory, yet it is an architecture recently built and inhabited.

Put another way, a building/architecture is
built for the programme of a Jewish School in
Berlin. In its naming, already a momentous
statement takes place, and it functions as a
school, celebrating the hope of the future, it is
a profound moment, a pivotal affirmation, a
moment of determination and joy, a strong,
living reality. Still, the memory of the past
must be kept in the inhabitants' minds and in
those outside of the school. The architecture
of the school keeps its promise through its
fact of existent reality, of its programme and
its memory of the past, the latter revealed
mysteriously in certain black, white and grey
photographs by Helene Binet. The covenant of
the architecture's soul and memory is revealed
through the space of her photographs, that is,
they capture an instant of time from which the
stillness and soundlessness make one
remember the past, an essential condition for
the existence of a future where life and
freedom can exist ... and evil is crushed.

THE BUILDING OF THE SCHOOL

ZVI HECKER

The school was designed in the form of a flower, as a gift to the children of Berlin. The sunflower's celestial construction seemed most suitable for planning the school, since its seeds orbit the sun and the suns rays illuminate all of the schoolrooms.

Berlin accepted the gift and entrusted us with the work. To begin with, calculations had to be made of the sun's orbits and the length of all the sun's rays. When these were completed, construction could begin. Bricks were brought and laid one over the other. Walls rose and the building began to emerge.

In time it became evident that the school, whilst under construction was gradually transforming into an intricate city. Streets and paths followed the orbits and the infinitesimal traces of the sun's rays. The school's exterior moulded the city's interior into a mirror of the universe, a place where light and shadow intersect. Children loved it and the work continued.

The building was nearing completion when uncertainty arose. By now the construction resembled neither a sunflower nor a city but a book whose open pages carry the load of the construction. Building a book was not our guiding principle, and experts had to be consulted as to the cause of the continually mutating images.

Following a lengthy Talmudic debate the school was eventually found to be built correctly. It was acknowledged that the sunflower, when transplanted from the Holy Land to Berlin evolved naturally into a book. The experts declared that the transformation was unavoidable since the Book represented the only lot Jews were allowed to cultivate in the Diaspora.

The theory of natural evolution was further reinforced by an account from the Old Testament. Beth-Sefer, the Hebrew word for school, when translated literally means House of the Book. The important biblical/etymological evidence restored confidence in our work and paved the way to the completion of the construction.

The only ones oblivious to these transformations were the school children. They had to discover themselves how the sunflower absorbs the light into its deep cut canyons and reflects it upon the pages of an open book and how in turn the House of the Book becomes a city of streets, courtyards and places to hide.

It seems inevitable that the rapid pace of transformation will turn full circle and come to completion. Finally, what many have suspected, will be revealed—that the House of the Book is not a building of the School, but a landscape of our childhood dreams.

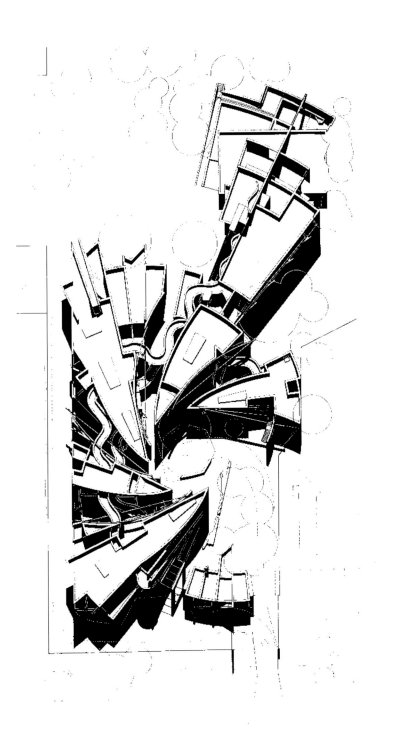

GROUND FLOOR PLAN

1. Main entrance
2. Secondary entrance
3. Classroom
4. Free time classroom
5. Corridor
6. Art workshop & laboratory
7. Library
8. Conference room
9. Administration

10. Headmaster
11. Staff room
12. Doctor's room
13. Store room
14. Mechanical room
15. Change & shower room
16. Gymnasium
17. Equipment room
18. Stands

19. Courtyard
20. Terrace
21. Play court
22. Entrance hall
23. Maintenance room
24. Auditorium & assembly hall
25. Gallery
26. Kitchen
27. Dining hall

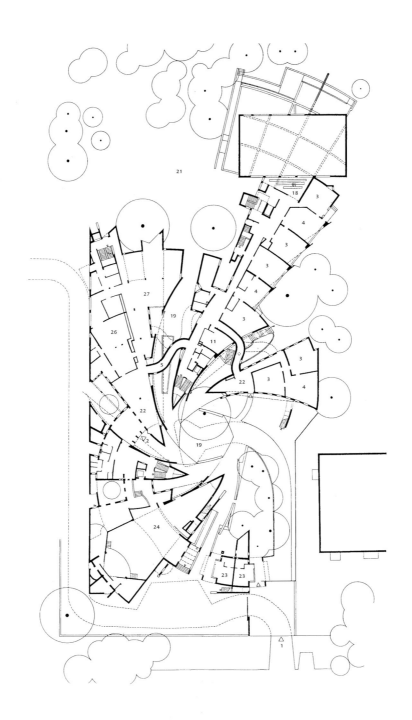

FIRST FLOOR PLAN

1. Main entrance
2. Secondary entrance
3. Classroom
4. Free time classrrom
5. Corridor
6. Art workshop & laboratory
7. Library
8. Conference room
9. Administration

10. Headmaster
11. Staff room
12. Doctor's room
13. Store room
14. Mechanical room
15. Change & shower room
16. Gymnasium
17. Equipment room
18. Stands

19. Courtyard
20. Terrace
21. Play court
22. Entrance hall
23. Maintenance room
24. Auditorium & assembly hall
25. Gallery
26. Kitchen
27. Dining hall

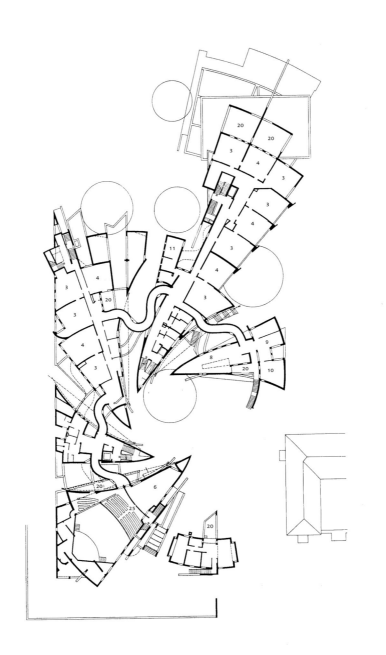

SECOND FLOOR PLAN

1. Main entrance
2. Secondary entrance
3. Classroom
4. Free time classroom
5. Corridor
6. Art workshop & laboratory
7. Library
8. Conference room
9. Administration

10. Headmaster
11. Staff room
12. Doctor's room
13. Store room
14. Mechanical room
15. Change & shower room
16. Gymnasium
17. Equipment room
18. Stands

19. Courtyard
20. Terrace
21. Play court
22. Entrance hall
23. Maintenance room
24. Auditorium & Assembly hall
25. Gallery
26. Kitchen
27. Dining hall

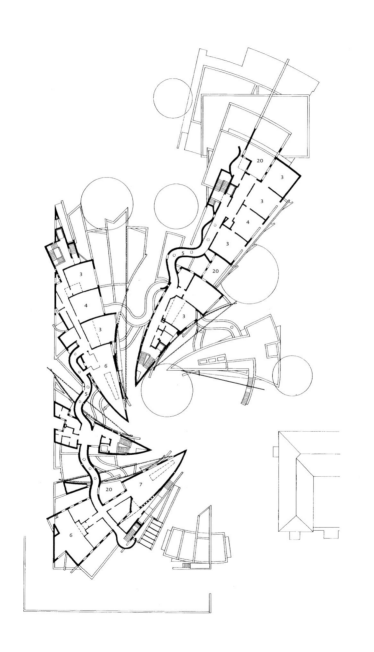

COLOPHON

Publisher
Black Dog
Publishing Limited
PO Box 3082
London NW1 UK

T. (44) 171 380 7500
F. (44) 171 380 7453
E. ucftlil@ucl.ac.uk

Design
Maria Beddoes and Paul Khera
Assisted by Amy Greenwood,
Mark Hutchinson, Mary Jackson,
Laura Mango, and Saxon Rawlings

Copy Editor
Maria Wilson

Printed in the European Union

© 1999 Black Dog Publishing Ltd &
Zvi Hecker, Helene Binet,
Peter Cook, John Hejduk

ISBN 1 901033 15 5